Dedicated to Cindy, who restores my faith in the natural order.

"Love is a subset of evolve. If we are to evolve, we must first learn how to love."
(Anonymous)

PROLOGUE

A Children's Book of African Animals from A-Z is an introduction to the study of animals or zoology. It is intended for older children with a well-established vocabulary and yet it is based on the same principles as the Dr. Seuss series of books. The use of imaginative rhyme, colorful illustrations, and repetition is a proven methodology for learning vocabulary and the retention of information. I utilize verse and illustrations as a means of capturing a child's imagination and hopefully stimulating a curiosity about the world of animals. I use both simple and sophisticated rhymes because it is my contention that children are capable of much more than we give them credit for. Some of the words used will undoubtedly prove to be unfamiliar and will require an explanation. As a parent, reading along with a child is one of life's simple pleasures. It is my hope that parents will enjoy this book as much as the children. The tone of this particular book is far more serious and much less humorous than *A Children's Book of Insects from A-Z,* which was the first in what will hopefully turn out to be, an entire series of children's books from A-Z. The reason for the change in tone is due to the seriousness of the subject. Unlike insects, African animals face an increasingly precarious future as their habitat shrinks. Africa is experiencing unprecedented changes due to rapid infrastructure development and ever-encroaching civilization. Nowhere in the world is the conflict between man and nature more evident. Many of Africa's animals are experiencing dwindling populations and the threat of extinction is a real possibility for some of the most magnificent and well-known animals on the planet. Hence, I broach subjects such as poaching as well as the violent nature of life and death in the animal kingdom. I have every confidence that a child's thirst for knowledge will engender a lifetime of interest in science and nature as well as a commitment to protect and preserve the flora and fauna which enrich our lives. G.D.

THE AARDVARK

Kingdom: Animalia

Phylum: Chordata

Class: Mammalia

Order: Tubulidentata

Family: Orycteropodidae

Genus: Orycteropus

Species: Orycteropus afer

I am an aardvark, I have a tongue long and sticky.

Finding enough food is always quite tricky.

Aardvarks have a pig-like nose, but we're not related.

Please don't call me a pig, it will leave me deflated.

Termites and ants are my favorite food source.

To me their demise is a matter of course.

If only I could find another ant hill!

I need to eat hundreds to have my fill.

When it comes to finding ants, I'm truly a wizard.

And just like the pangolin, I too, have a gizzard.

There are big differences between us, the pangolin has scales.

Whereas I have teeth, yet one more reason why, comparison fails.

In order to find them, I'll use my superb sense of smell.

My hearing is excellent, but I don't see things so well.

With powerful claws I rip up stumps or the ground.

Revealing beneath, the treasure I found.

The forefeet have four toes, whereas the rear feet have five.

My objective is to eat the ants, while they're still alive.

Once these insects are no longer concealed.

I'll slurp them up quickly, an adequate yield.

My appetite sated, I've had my fun.

While the survivors repair the damage I've done.

Is this the reason why I'm called a thug or a goon?

Or the way I'm portrayed in the Pink Panther cartoon?

I'm not handsome or pretty with such a long snout.

Some would say I'm ugly, but you won't see me pout.

The natural world needs me to perform the role I play.

So I don't pay attention to what others might say.

I dig several different types of burrows.

My permanent home features tunnels and furrows.

I use the burrows to escape the heat of the day.

I'll wait until nighttime, before I come out to play.

When I no longer use them, other animals move in.

There they find refuge for themselves as well as their kin.

THE BABOON

Kingdom: Animalia

Phylum: Chordata

Class: Mammalia

Order: Primates

Suborder: Haplorhini

Infraorder: Simiiformes

Family: Cercopithecidae

Tribe: Papionini

Genus: Papio

I'm a baboon, but you won't find me alone.

A solitary life I cannot condone.

We baboons live in tight-knit, social groups.

From five to two hundred fifty, is the size of our troops.

With dog-like muzzles and close-set eyes.

We vary in weight and differ in size.

Though our short tails, buttocks, and muzzles are bare.

The rest of our bodies are covered in hair.

We are omnivorous, but mostly eat plants.

Quite often passive, with occasional rants.

Our life span is about 30 years in the wild.

45 in captivity, if raised like a child.

Although we are often noisy and loud.

Baboon parents are doting and proud.

One of our favorite pastimes is social grooming.

It helps us to bond when danger is looming.

Baboons can raise a call for alarm.

When predators near and mean them harm.

A similar call signals a challenge between males.

The troop will remain edgy when compromise fails.

When two males blink fast and begin to yawn.

It's an obvious threat until one of them is gone.

Into this dispute, an infant is drawn.

The mother howls, while it's used as a pawn.

What causes a male to grab a baboon baby?

The infant is used as a live shield maybe?

The male baboon doesn't feel any shame.

Baboons are wild and they are far from tame.

THE CHEETAH

Kingdom: Animalia

Phylum: Chordata

Class: Mammalia

Order: Carnivora

Suborder: Feliformia

Family: Felinae

Genus: Acinonyx

Species: Acinonyx jubatus

I am a cheetah and I am incredibly fast.

Though I am quick, my speed doesn't last.

If I cannot catch something quick due to my haste.

My time and energy spent will be a waste.

I have got to creep close to my prey.

Otherwise, they just might get away.

Like other cats, there are spots all over my fur.

They help me to blend in or my image to blur.

I am unique among cats, with non-retractable claws.

As I creep forward, I silently pause.

I'll choose one animal apart from the herd.

It's all that I need, I give you my word.

I catch the old, young, sick or weak.

These are the less fleet animals I seek.

A tasty antelope would provide delight.

While the rest of the herd would take off in fright.

I zero in on the one I think I can catch.

Speed against speed, it has met its match.

When I am close, I'll use my claws.

Cause it to stumble, then use my jaws.

When I bite, I go for the throat.

Once it's lifeless, then I can gloat.

I'll drag it away, conceal my kill.

I must eat quickly, have my fill.

Scavengers will try to steal it away.

I'll do my best to keep them at bay.

After I've eaten, then I can lie down and rest.

Renew my energy, thanks to the meat I digest.

THE DESERT WARTHOG

Kingdom: Animalia

Phylum: Chordata

Class: Mammalia

Order: Artiodactyla

Family: Suidae

Genus: Phacochoerus

Species: Phacochoerus aethiopicus

Desert warthogs are a species thought to be extinct.

Later discovered to be genetically linked.

We have protuberances on each side of the face.

Which is why we are called warthogs, but they are not a disgrace.

Our outward appearance draws many stares.

Our bodies covered by bristling hairs.

The hair is denser along the spine and forms a mid to dark brown crest.

Grasses, leafy plants, flowers, and fruit are some of the things I ingest.

Do you remember *Pumba* from *The Lion King?*

It seems as though he would eat almost anything.

Our sources of food are often far-flung.

Yes, we are known to sometimes eat dung.

Our tusks are large, curved, canine teeth.

They appear to protrude from the jawbone beneath.

Our range is centered on a watering hole.

A year-round source of water is the ultimate goal.

Warthogs are unwilling hosts of the tsetse fly.

A parasitic insect, I wish they'd all die.

These flies act as a vector of sleeping sickness.

But don't seem to affect our appetite or quickness.

We dig burrows so we can live underground.

There aren't any safer places yet to be found.

To a litter of two or three piglets, a female with give birth.

They will follow the mother closely when they're of sufficient girth.

Males are invariably larger, with a stocky build.

Warthogs are quick to run away, before they are killed.

They all make a dash for the burrows, the piglets dive headfirst.

The adults back in, tusks outward, their tempers at their worst.

Desert warthogs form groups of mainly females and offspring called sounders.

Adult males are solitary, one hundred and sixty-five pounders.

Desert warthogs are not endangered, in fact, quite prolific.

Their numbers are stable, but I can't be specific.

THE ELEPHANT

Kingdom: Animalia

Phylum: Chordata

Subphylum: Vertebrata

Class: Mammalia

Superorder: Afrotheria

Order: Proboscidea

Family: Elephantidae

I am an elephant, social and smart.

The herd is my family and we're never apart.

I am also known as a pachyderm.

I'll forgive you, if you don't know this term.

You'll recognize me by my impressive trunk and large ears.

We elephants can live from sixty to seventy years.

Elephants have ivory tusks in off-white.

One of the reasons for the elephants' plight.

We have the ability to think and to reason.

Our favorite time of year is the rainy season.

We walk many miles in search of food and water.

The summers seem to be drier and hotter.

Our lives often filled with suffering and pain.

Is it any wonder why we welcome the rain?

Elephants are gentle creatures, though they are massive.

Often exploited by humans because we're so passive.

We are treated like slaves for circus entertainment.

Sometimes mistreated, a sad and captive arrangement.

While our movements are rather cautious and slow.

When I am angry, I can deliver a blow.

Not to be trusted, our feet shackled by chains.

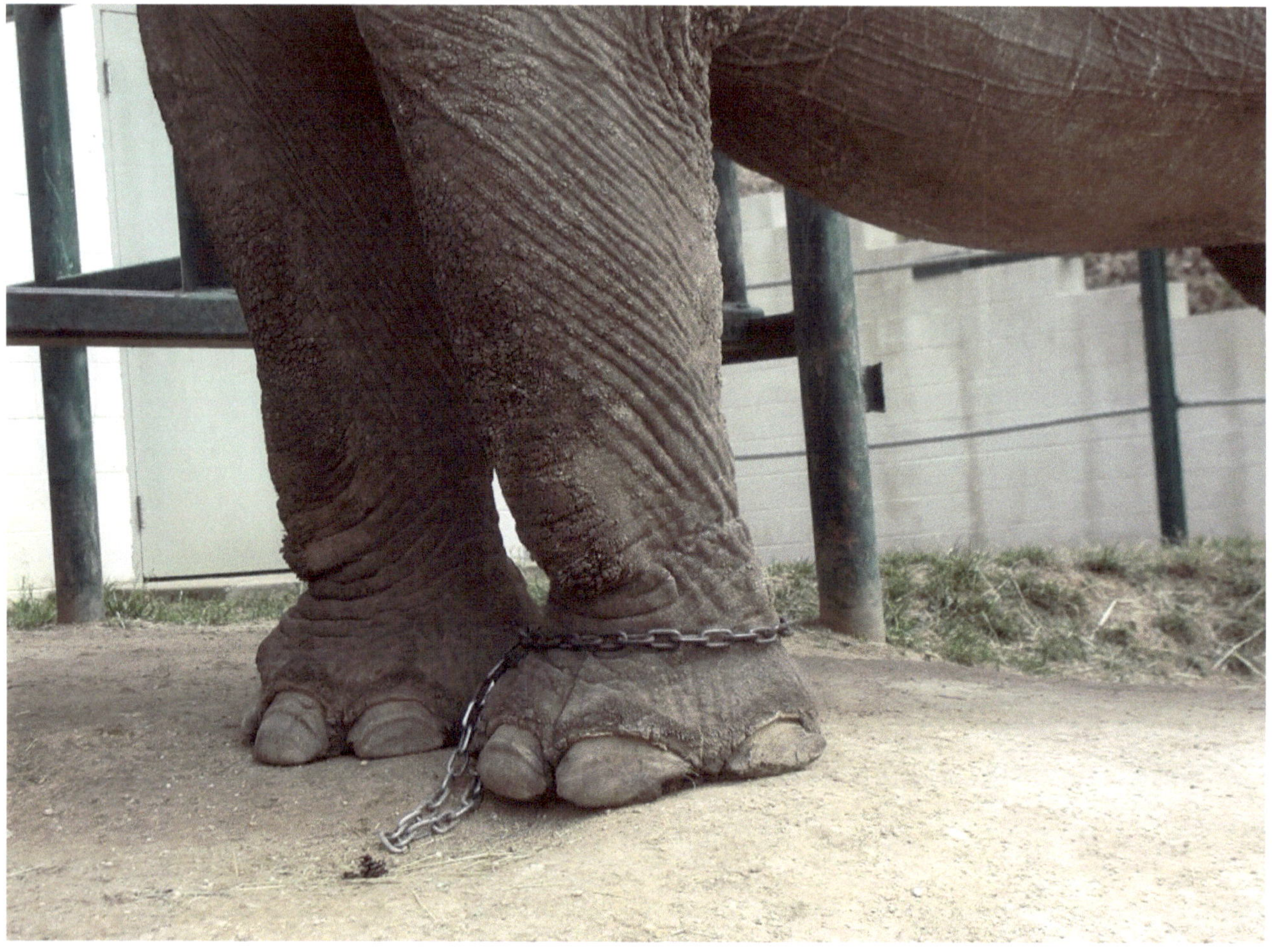

The tricks we perform are for monetary gains.

Some novelty items include elephant art.

Paint smeared on canvas, does it come straight from the heart?

Don't fall for this gimmick, it's only a trick.

The paintings sell for thousands, it makes me sick.

Many elephants were slaughtered during the ivory trade.

Poachers still willing to take risks for the money to be made.

Protected by treaty, the trade in ivory has ceased.

Though the black market is thriving, thanks to the palms that are greased.

Too little, too late for the elephants deceased.

Who, in their right mind, can kill such a magnificent beast?

They say that an elephant never forgets.

We mourn our dead with deepest regrets.

THE FENNEC FOX

Kingdom: Animalia

Phylum: Chordata

Class: Mammalia

Order: Carnivora

Family: Canidae

Genus: Vulpes

Species: Vulpes zerda

The fennec fox is nocturnal and small.

The average size is only eight inches tall.

We are the smallest of foxes, but have extremely large ears.

We can live in captivity for up to fourteen years.

Our ears give us an acute sense of hearing.

We use this sense to detect prey that is nearing.

The other advantage is that they dissipate heat.

As omnivores we aren't fussy about the things that we eat.

Our kidneys allow us to survive with minimal water.

We live in the desert where conditions are hotter.

We feed on insects, rodents, rabbits, and eggs.

A fennec fox has a brown coat, a tail, and four legs.

Fennec foxes are known to mate for life.

Raise their young, like a husband and wife.

We rear our kits in large dens, dug in the sand.

Another example of how we live off the land.

 Our blood vessels are located close to the skin.

We live in packs near the rest of our kin.

Most other foxes live solitary lives.

These foxes would die, whereas the fennec survives.

THE GIRAFFE

Kingdom: Animalia

Phylum: Chordata

Class: Mammalia

Order: Artiodactyla

Family: Giraffidae

Genus: Giraffa

Species: Giraffa Camelopardalis

You'll recognize me by my neck, which is long.

If you think I eat meat, then you are wrong.

I eat the leaves from the tallest of trees.

I can reach wherever I please.

We are the largest animals known to digest food by rumination.

Which is the breakdown of plant-foods by the process of fermentation.

Giraffes also feature a blue-black tongue.

The ground is fertilized by piles of our dung.

Giraffes are the tallest living terrestrial, or land creature.

Our long necks are certainly the most identifiable feature.

Our height and keen eyesight provide a unique point of view.

Our unique pattern of markings vary in shape, size, and hue.

On the top of our heads are short and stubby ossicones.

Protuberances of horn, or more likely, antler-like bones.

Only about half of giraffes will become an adult.

Predation is the principal reason for the result.

Aside from the lion, adult giraffes have nothing to worry about.

Against smaller predators, our size and our strength will always win out.

Only male giraffes engage in mild to serious necking.

A contest of strength, a competitor's plans for the wrecking.

We'll bang our necks together, as hard as we can.

To drive off our rival, is the ultimate plan.

While there is no argument that giraffe populations are in a sad state.

The number of giraffe species and subspecies is a matter of debate.

THE HYENA

Kingdom: Animalia

Phylum: Chordata

Class: Mammalia

Order: Carnivora

Suborder: Feliformia

Infraorder: Viverroidea

Family: Hyaenidae

Genera: Crocuta, Hyaena, and Proteles

Striped, brown, and spotted are the three species of hyenas.

I'll try to remain impartial to what they are seen as.

Scoundrels, villians, demons, murderers, you take your pick.

The tales of their evil are enough to make one sick.

Hyenas have characteristics of both dog and cat.

Two common enemies, can you imagine that!

Spotted hyenas can crunch bones into pieces.

When day turns to night, the danger increases.

Spotted hyenas kill ninety-five percent of what they eat.

They rarely need to scavenge at night, for their sources of meat.

It must be terrifying to listen to them in the dark.

In the nearby African villages, the terror is stark.

Many villagers have reportedly been dragged off as prey.

Never again to see their loved ones or the light of day.

While the brown and the striped hyenas are less of a threat.

The pages of a book are as close as I'll ever get.

Hyenas have earned a bad reputation.

By virtue of attacks and mutilation.

We are opportunists, we eat what we can.

Killing or stealing is part of our plan.

Some of our group will act as a distraction.

So that others can execute this plan of action.

It makes no difference to us what we attack.

It all depends on whether it fights back.

Old and sick or perhaps a newborn calf.

The kill is enough to make us laugh.

We have even been known to take on a lion.

As long as none of us are left injured and dyin'.

Although the hippopotamus and hyena share the same letter.

The joke is on the hippos, because we hyenas are much better.

We wouldn't be foolish enough for an adult hippo to tackle.

But if we can ambush a baby one, we will begin to cackle.

Some people are offended by the way hyenas giggle.

You would laugh out loud too, if you saw a big, fat hippo wiggle.

In all seriousness, we hyenas are often wrongly portrayed.

The respect for our strength and cunning has been far too long delayed.

Hyenas are very important to African ecology.

If I gave you a bad impression, I owe you an apology.

THE IMPALA

Kingdom: Animalia

Phylum: Chordata

Class: Mammalia

Order: Artiodactyla

Family: Bovidae

Subfamily: Aepycerotinae

Genus: Aepyceros

Species: Aepyceros melampus

An impala is an antelope, of medium size.

Always on the alert for the predators, we most despise.

The two species of impalas are the common and black-faced.

The impala's leaping and running is very fast paced.

Only the males have horns slender and curved.

They use them to see an opponent unnerved.

These horns are also ridged and shaped like a lyre. (Pronounced: lahyuh r or liar)

When fully grown, they are a sight to admire.

The common impala has black streaks down both the hind legs.

What differentiates the black-faced, is the question it begs.

They have black streaks on each side of the face and right down the middle.

If you consider yourself an expert, then answer my riddle.

Whenever I roar, do I keep my mouth wide open or closed?

The latter is the correct answer for the question I posed.

One to three snorts can be heard a great distance, over a mile away.

Remember sound travels farther at night than in the heat of the day.

Our teeth are arranged like a fine-toothed comb.

There are ticks present wherever we roam.

Impalas are known to engage in frequent attempts at self-grooming.

Especially during times when tick populations are booming.

We have also been known to groom each other.

When one patch is tick-free, we move to another.

Once impalas are reasonably clean.

They can focus on remaining unseen.

The black-faced impalas are fewer in number.

A vulnerable species, one not to encumber.

THE JACKAL

Kingdom: Animalia

Phylum: Chordata

Class: Mammalia

Order: Carnivora

Family: Canidae

Genus: Canis

The jackal is an animal, very much maligned.

To call someone a jackal, is certainly unkind.

Medium in stature, a maximum of twenty inches in height.

Jackals have sharp canine teeth, we can kill with just one bite.

Omnivorous scavengers, though our diet is meat.

We can run long distances, in dry, desert heat.

The African jackals are side-striped or black-backed.

Our vocal sounds pack specific, a little known fact.

Black-backed and side-striped jackals are monogamous, which means they have one mate.

The male and female will stay together, in an effort to procreate.

From ten to thirty, is the relative size of our nearby packs.

Unlike our cousins the wolves, we tend to avoid mass attacks.

Jackals are nocturnal, we are mostly active at night.

We hunt alone or in pairs, until the dawn's early light.

THE KUDU

Kingdom: Animalia

Phylum: Chordata

Class: Mammalia

Order: Artiodactyla

Family: Bovidae

Subfamily: Bovinae

Genus: Tragelaphus

Species: Tragelaphus strepsiceros (Greater Kudu)

       Tragelaphus imberbis (Lesser Kudu)

The two species of kudu are the lesser and greater.

I'm not sure which one came sooner and which one came later.

There are also subspecies, it depends on the region.

In the African woodlands, the kudus were once legion.

Thanks to farming activity, the woodland habitat is shrinking.

Although better irrigation has added to sources for drinking.

With drinking water abundant in unlikely places.

The kudus are settling in more inhabited spaces.

On the kudus' torsos are vertical stripes, four to twelve.

In case you are interested, and want to further delve.

The horns have two and a half, to as many as three twists.

They are as long as your arms and as thick as your wrists.

Adult bulls' throats are covered by hairy manes.

Much less vocal, when the urge to rut wanes.

Our diet consists of leaves, grass, and shoots.

Occasionally tubers, fruit, and roots.

We are especially fond of tangerines.

We prefer oranges much more than greens.

As large as we are, we can't outrun our foes.

Easily overtaken, when one of us slows.

But with powerful kicks, we defend our own lives.

And if one of us should lose, the rest of the herd thrives.

THE LION

Kingdom: Animalia

Phylum: Chordata

Class: Mammalia

Order: Carnivora

Suborder: Feliformia

Family: Felidae

Subfamily: Pantherinae

Genus: Panthera

Species: Panthera leo

I am a lion, considered by many a king.

I wonder what food the lioness will bring?

She does the hunting while I wait behind.

I will eat first, I hope she won't mind.

A tender gazelle or a plump wildebeest.

Would make a tasty treat or a kingly feast.

You'll recognize me by my thick, flowing mane.

Few are willing to challenge my reign.

A group of lions is called a pride.

We wander the veld, no reason to hide.

And if you were to hear me roar.

I would make your heart rate soar!

Only hyenas don't seem afraid.

They fear not, the noise that I've made.

Sometimes I'll try to chase them away.

Before they steal the flesh of my prey.

I realize hyenas have to eat too.

But they are many while we are few.

Why can't they find their own food to eat?

Defeating these thieves is no easy feat.

The top of the food chain is a good place to be.

I eat other animals before they eat me.

Don't bother the king or steal the bones that he gnaws.

I have sharp teeth and razor-like claws.

Lions can kill with one swipe of our paws.

There's no escape from our mighty jaws.

No longer hungry, I lie in the shade.

As king of the beasts, I've got it made.

THE MEERKAT

Kingdom: Animalia

Phylum: Chordata

Class: Chordata

Order: Carnivora

Family: Herpestidae

Genus: Suricata

With long, slender limbs, a tail, and feet with just four toes.

Our faces somewhat tapered, toward a cute, brown nose.

You might remember me from the popular T.V. show.

We were given names, but mine I don't know.

"Meerkat Manor" is an intimate look at meerkat life.

Triumphant and tragic, the rewards and the strife.

A relative of the mongoose, a meerkat is nimble and agile.

Subject to social complexity and danger, a life very fragile.

A group of meerkats is called a mob, gang or clan.

We welcome new arrivals, but some we will ban.

Sometimes these outcasts get lucky and will join a new mob.

They will be given new status, a new role, a new job.

There is always one sentry on duty to sound the alarm.

Meerkats are trained to take turns, to keep the mob safe from harm.

On its hind legs, the sentry stands tall.

Ready and willing to make the call.

The sentry will tell us if the threat is coming from the land or the air.

Whether it's a cobra snake or a hungry hawk, we'll be aware.

The vocal sounds include a chirrup, bark, growl or trill.

They signal when to panic, as well as when to chill.

From certain types of venom, meerkats have become immune.

But when bitten by a cobra, death comes all too soon.

THE NYALA

Kingdom: Animalia

Phylum: Chordata

Class: Mammalia

Order: Artiodactyla

Family: Bovidae

Subfamily: Bovinae

Genus: Nyala also considered to be in the genus Tragelaphus

Species: Tragelaphus angasii or Nyala angasii

The nyala is an antelope, which can live for up to nineteen years.

Lowland woodlands and thickets, are the places the nyala appears.

Females and juveniles have vertical stripes, ten or more.

Like other antelope, the nyala is an herbivore.

Females and juveniles vary in color, from rusty to rufous brown.

The males have spiral horns upon their heads, yellow-tipped, just like a crown.

Older males are solitary, others forming groups up to ten.

Females and their offspring, bachelor males depending on when.

Hairy glands on the feet, leave a scent wherever the nyala walks.

One would think it would be so easy to track, when a predator stalks.

THE ORYX

Kingdom: Animalia

Phylum: Chordata

Class: Mammalia

Order: Artiodactyla

Family: Bovidae

Subfamily: Hippotraginae

Genus: Oryx

Species: Oryx gazella, Oryx beisa, and Oryx dammah

There are four species called oryxes, but only three are native to Africa.

If you don't believe me, consult the Encyclopedia Brittanica.

One should be able to recognize, the oryx without fail.

There are dark markings on the face and legs, yet the body is pale.

Up to six hundred oryxes, can be found in a herd.

There is safety in numbers, oryxes will not be deterred.

The oryx is one of the largest and most powerful antelopes.

Its future far from certain, its survival is one of my hopes.

Few predators are willing to take on, an oryx in its prime.

The oryx can survive without water, for long periods of time.

An animal's strength and stamina, are important in times of dearth.

A newborn oryx is able to run, immediately after birth.

Unlike other antelopes, the oryxes' horns are straight and long.

They use them for self-defense, or when others try to do them wrong.

It's a more difficult proposition, to tell apart the sexes.

Both of them have permanent horns, an observation which perplexes.

The oryx is not averse, to using its horns readily.

Predators often learn far too late, that these horns are deadly.

Lions have been known to attack, and they themselves are killed.

For the oryx is formidable, in addition to strong-willed.

Hunting oryxes as a prize game trophy, is, a dubious distinction.

Some species of oryxes, have already been hunted, to near extinction.

THE PANGOLIN

Kingdom: Animalia

Phylum: Chordata

Class: Mammalia

Clade: Scrotifera

Clade: Fereuungulata

(Unranked): Ferre

Order: Pholidota

Family: Manidae

Genera: Phataginus and Smutsia

The pangolin is a prehistoric, scaly anteater.

As African animals go, there are few that are neater.

When I am threatened, I usually curl up in a ball.

Most give up without anything, to show for it at all.

The scales overlap one another and form a hardened shell.

Where my head starts and where my tail ends, is often hard to tell.

The scales are made of keratin, like claws or fingernails.

When competing for a female, males will flail their tails.

Pangolins can emit a noxious-smelling gunk.

From glands near the anus, similar to a skunk.

Pangolins are unable to chew, because of their lack of teeth.

Powerful claws rip up the ground, to find ants or termites beneath.

Their exceptionally long, sticky tongues, are invariably thin.

Probing for ant or termite colonies, in tunnels deep within.

Pangolins are picky, only one to two species of insects will do.

They utilize small stones in their gizzards to grind the ants into goo.

With a poor sense of vision, but excellent smell and hearing.

The pangolin's appearance is nevertheless endearing.

The pangolin is reputed to be an excellent swimmer.

They are mostly nocturnal, or most active when light is dimmer.

Although shy and secretive, they are an easy prize.

Traffickers don't care, if the pangolin lives or dies.

Over one hundred thousand pangolins are smuggled every year.

That statistic should bother you, enough to shed a tear.

THE LETTER 'Q'

There are no African animals that begin with a 'Q'.

Though most of the ones mentioned, can be found at the zoo.

Many of them will need a larger enclosure.

To make them comfortable and prevent exposure.

It's a crime to confine a wild animal in a cage.

Their mental health is often difficult to gauge.

The ones who repeat movements over and over again.

Deserve a change of scenery or a much larger pen.

I've witnessed polar bears rub against rocks till they bled.

If only they could talk, they'd say they're better off dead.

Wild animals range many miles at their leisure.

To deny them their freedom, is a cost beyond measure.

Their dignity, sanity, and joie de vie. (Pronounced: zhwa-de-vee)

The price animals pay for our entrance fee.

Do animals have a joie de vivre? (Pronounced zhwa-de-veev')

It all depends on what you believe.

Wild animals in zoos often live longer.

Due to their diet, they're physically stronger.

I suppose some people consider this fact a success.

Their quality of life is diminished, nevertheless.

In the state of New Hampshire, they say "live free or die".

It's the same for wild animals, a rallying cry.

Not all zoos are bad, although I've seen my share.

The good ones treat animals with love and care.

THE RHINOCEROS

Kingdom: Animalia

Phylum: Chordata

Class: Mammalia

Order: Perissodactyla

Subfamily: Rhinocerotoidea

I am a rhinoceros, the short form is rhino.

We are categorized as black, white or albino.

My vision is poor, I can scarcely see.

I'm ill-tempered, so stay away from me.

I don't mind the oxpecker bird as it rests on my back.

It eats the parasitic bugs, which often attack.

My hide is hard to penetrate, as it is strong and thick.

For an animal my size, I am amazingly quick.

I have few enemies, so I have no fear.

Yet our numbers are dwindling with each passing year.

A group of rhinos is called a crash.

It is with humans that we often clash.

If I end up extinct, my loss you shall mourn.

All because of my highly sought-after horn.

In Asian markets, they grind my horn into powder.

For those who protect me, I couldn't be prouder.

I am disgusted by anyone who poaches.

I regard them as nothing but human cockroaches.

One would expect an herbivore to be rather docile.

I'm sorry to say, my temperament is often hostile.

Please excuse me, if your vehicle I tend to jostle.

However, one should remember, I'm a living fossil.

Rhinos were featured in the Hollywood movie called *"Hatari"*.

They were captured alive by men on an African safari.

The rhinos were captured so they could be sold to zoos.

It was a dangerous job for the camera crews.

John Wayne was the only actor tough enough to play the lead role.

He had to capture rhinos with only a rope and a pole.

THE SERVAL

Kingdom: Animalia

Phylum: Chordata

Class: Mammalia

Order: Carnivora

Suborder: Feliformia

Family: Felidae

Subfamily: Felinae

Genus: Leptailurus

Species: Leptailurus serval

The serval is a solitary, wild, African cat.

Its body lean, slender, and muscular, not at all fat.

Our diet consists of rodents, insects, a reptile or frog.

One of the servals' enemies is the African wild dog.

A beautiful cat with a golden-yellow to buff coat.

Its black spots, stripes, and short tail are also worthy of note.

With keen sight, smell, and hearing, servals leap on their prey.

They trap it with their forefeet, so it won't get away.

Next comes a bite to the neck or the head.

It's all over quickly, the creature is dead.

Can you imagine the serval as a house pet?

Is this a decision one might come to regret?

Guaranteed to make tongues wag and neighbors to gawk.

I guess the neighborhood dogs will be in for a shock!

Servals have the longest legs of any cat, relative to size.

I am not so sure that having a serval, as a pet, is wise.

Servals grow to twenty-four inches tall and forty pounds in weight.

Owning a wild animal causes a great deal of debate.

Provided servals are well taken care of, I don't see the harm.

All this wonderful cat needs, is a loving home or a farm.

THOMSON'S GAZELLE

Kingdom: Animalia

Phylum: Chordata

Class: Mammalia

Order: Artiodactyla

Family: Bovidae

Subfamily: Antelopinae

Genus: Eudorcas

Species: Eudorcas thomsonii

The Thomson's gazelle is fleet of foot.

But when we graze, the herd stays put.

We gazelles rely on safety in numbers.

One stands guard while another one slumbers.

The stomp of a hoof is all that it'll take.

To spook the herd and make the ground shake.

We take off running in the blink of an eye.

We've escaped danger until there's a cry.

A young gazelle, from the herd was singled out.

Caught by a cheetah, its survival in doubt.

No time to look back, we've made our escape.

Such is life on the African Cape.

THE LETTER 'U'

There are no African animals that begin with a 'U'.

I know it's hard to believe, but I swear it's true.

Africa was known as "The Dark Continent".

I've never been there, a fact I lament.

They say the sights, the sounds, and the smell of the earth.

Leave a lasting impression, a sense of rebirth.

In the African wild, there's no imposed morality.

No right, no wrong, life and death in its totality.

THE VERVET MONKEY

Kingdom: Animalia

Phylum: Chordata

Class: Mammalia

Order: Primates

Suborder: Haplorhini

Infraorder: Simiiformes

Family: Cercopithecidae

Genus: Chlorocebus

Species: Chlorocebus pygerythrus

The vervet monkey, or simply the vervet for short.

Has five subspecies of a slightly different sort.

The vervet has a black face with a fringe of white hair over the eyes.

Their complex vocalizations are a series of calls, screams, and cries.

They form different groups, due to a number of factors.

They can mimic behavior, like a troupe of actors.

The vervet monkey often serves as a nonhuman primate model.

Their behavior is similar to humans, their offspring they'll coddle.

The infants typically receive a tremendous amount of attention.

From immature females and grandmothers, according to social convention.

The grandmother's presence often leads to a greater vitality.

Which has been associated with decreased infant mortality.

Biomedical research has proven statistics.

That vervet monkeys exhibit human characteristics.

It is a rare occurrence to witness animals acting out of spite.

Yet a vervet can destroy the food of another without taking a bite.

A vervet's diet consists mostly of fruit, leaves, flowers, and seeds.

Though there is a naughty aspect to the way a vervet feeds.

In farming areas, they feed on crops and are considered pests.

They have also been observed to steal eggs and chicks from their nests.

Vervet monkeys have exhibited hypertension and anxiety.

And when they are introduced to alcohol, a lack of sobriety.

The vervet monkey has a social system, fragile and complex.

Hierarchical dominance represented by either sex.

By studying animals, you can learn a lot about yourself.

The accumulation of knowledge is a measure of wealth.

THE WILDEBEEST

Kingdom: Animalia

Phylum: Chordata

Class: Mammalia

Order: Artiodactyla

Family: Bovidae

Subfamily: Alcelaphinae

Genus: Connochaetes

Species: Connochaetes gnou (Black Wikdebeest)

Connochaetes taurinus (Blue Wildebeest)

Wildebeests come in species black and blue.

A wildebeest is sometimes called a gnu.

From a distance, we resemble oxen or cattle.

Though we are sturdily built and ready for battle.

With broad muzzles, thick horns, and wide roman noses.

We can deliver a blow, if one opposes.

Our muscular legs are even toed.

Able to carry a heavy load.

Wildebeests weigh from three hundred-forty to over five hundred-fifty pounds.

We are known to heed baboons' as well as other animals' alarm call sounds.

Some wildebeests are migratory, while others are sedentary.

It depends on species and habitat, it's really elementary.

Sometimes nomadic, which just means that we wander.

Always in search of a better place over yonder.

We hang out with zebras, on open grasslands.

It's the type of habitat which meets our demands.

An abundance of food and a good field of vision.

Come in handy when we make a split second decision.

Living alongside zebras is a matter of trust.

We rely on their awareness, their keen senses a must.

We all follow suit if one takes off running.

It means a predator is near, sly and cunning.

The sound of our hooves is as loud as thunder.

We hope that one of us won't be torn asunder.

We make our escape in a cloud of dust.

Acutely aware of the predator's blood lust.

To flee is the best way to survive when attacked.

It takes a while to calm down when your heart rate is jacked.

Zebras and wildebeests seek mutual protection.

By virtue of each other's sense of detection.

THE LETTER 'X'

There are no African animals that begin with an 'X'.

But for those animals poached, let us pay our respects.

Poaching animals is an illegal activity.

A reflection of poverty and lack of civility.

The killing of animals for food can be forgiven.

But the poaching of animals is economically driven.

Poachers tend to be poor while their clients are wealthy.

The end result is animal populations less healthy.

Some are already extinct while others are in danger.

So too is the life of the African park ranger.

Outnumbered by poachers and often outgunned.

Please donate to the African wildlife fund.

Why is mankind so inherently destructive?

I'll try to answer in a manner deductive.

It is the nature of man to change the environment.

Technological advancement is a fundamental requirement.

The more we advance, the more damage is done.

From fire to the spear, from the bow to the gun.

Animals kill instinctively and keep nature in balance.

While developing weapons is one of man's inherent talents.

Our existence precarious in this atomic age.

No lessons are learned from the wars we wage.

THE LETTER 'Y'

There are no African animals that begin with a 'Y'.

Allow me to explain why some live and some die.

Survival of the fittest is nature's rule.

At first glance, this seems to be cruel.

Only the smartest and strongest survive.

They ensure that the species shall thrive.

Life is often short for the young, the old, the sick, and the weak.

It may seem like a tragedy with a future so bleak.

Yet life goes on as it always does.

Though not quite the same as it once was.

THE ZEBRA

Kingdom: Animalia

Phylum: Chordata

Class: Mammalia

Order: Perissodactyla

Family: Equidae

Genus: Equus

Subgenus: Hippotigris & Dolichohippus

Species: Equus zebra, Equus quagga, and Equus grevyi

Am I white with black stripes or am I black with white?

If you answered black with white stripes, then you'd be right.

Just like fingerprints, every zebra has a unique set of stripes.

Vertical or horizontal, there are two different types.

Can zebras use these stripes to identify one another?

A father from a mother or a sister from a brother?

No one really knows for sure, the purpose that they serve.

I will list all of them, in the order they deserve.

Studies have shown that zebras attract far fewer flies.

Another theory is the stripes mask the shape and the size.

Once the zebra is in motion, stripes can serve to confuse or fool.

The final theory is that the stripes help the zebra to stay cool.

Zebras can walk, trot, canter or gallop, four distinct types of gaits.

Another example of the zebra's uniquely equine traits.

Zebras have excellent sight and hearing, their sense of taste and smell acute.

So do many of the zebra's enemies, so the point is really moot.

When a zebra is cornered, it will put up a fight.

They can fend off an attack, by a kick or a bite.

This group of zebras is called a harem, one stallion, plus mares and foals.

To challenge a breeding stallion, is one of the bachelor male's goals.

Groups of zebras are referred to as a herd, dazzle, or zeal.

How a person should refer to these groups is really no big deal.

People have tried and failed, in their attempts to tame me.

A seemingly impossible task, as I'm wild and free.

Attempts have ended in futility, no matter how they try.

Zebras are far too high-strung to give in, they would rather die.

The plains zebras are plentiful, while the mountain and grevyi are not.

The quagga became extinct long ago, which is why children must be taught.

A MESSAGE OF THANKS

I hope you enjoyed this book about animals, written entirely in verse.

How could it have been better or what could have possibly made it worse?

When I set out to complete this project, I had to think of words that rhyme.

Composing coherent sentences, takes an inordinate amount of time.

Your feedback is important, so please feel free to let me know.

If your feedback is positive, this series of books will surely grow.

EPILOGUE (INTENDED FOR PARENTS)

As a young boy, a trip to the zoo was a unique opportunity to enjoy the sights, sounds, and smells of animals from all over the world. The largest and most fascinating were the African animals and I took great delight in feeding peanuts to the elephants, amazed by the dexterity of their trunks. My father captured some of these moments at the zoo with an 8mm movie camera and the recorded images reveal a child at play in a much simpler world. Times have changed. Most zoos place greater restrictions on the interaction of people and animals, understandably so. A healthy diet and exercise regimen are critical for the health and longevity of animals. The other and no less important reason for restricting contact between people and animals, is to limit the possibility of litigation in an increasingly litigious world. The life expectancy of animals in captivity often far exceeds that of an animal in the wild. Whether or not the quality of life is enhanced is a matter of debate. Repetitive and monotonous behavior, boredom, and self-inflicted injuries or abuse would suggest otherwise. The preeminent beasts of Africa are especially vulnerable and scientists, as usual, promise solutions and a bright future based on their chosen field of expertise. I am extremely skeptical, as science continues to be elevated to the status of a religion. The salvation of mankind and solutions to our problems have long been prophesied by Marxists, Scientologists, and their ilk. I recall watching a slick presentation featuring some of the world's leading scientific experts and futurists. Their ebullient prognostications included the eradication of poverty, the redefinition of work, the realization of everyone's potential and productivity, the guarantee of personal fulfilment, harmony between humanity and nature, etc. They painted a picture eerily similar to that of the utopian socialists of the past. However, when I viewed another short presentation about how scientists would accomplish the task of species survival, I was struck by the lack of consensus among them. For example, geneticists argued that their efforts could perpetuate species well after they become extinct. Other scientists argued that without the preservation of their habitat, the essence of the species would be lost. There is no question that we are on the precipice of revolutionary change. I am also aware that revolution is, by nature, chaotic and bloody.

While there is nothing wrong with science and technology per se, technological advancements haven't made our lives any easier, despite promises to that effect. If anything, science and technology tend to make our lives more complicated. These advancements always seem to be both a blessing and a curse. Computers are powerful tools, but rife with malicious viruses. 3D printers have been used to design composite firearms which are difficult to detect by airport x-ray machines. Scientists and engineers have created brighter, energy efficient LED lights. However, these brighter lights are disrupting natural patterns of sleep, especially in urban environments. Arrogant scientists and engineers have succeeded in harnessing the wind and, more importantly, the power of the sun. The deleterious results are dead birds of prey (raptors), weapons of mass destruction, Three Mile Island, Chernobil, and Fukushima. We are witnessing the extinction of animals and, perhaps, the extinction of mankind. My hope is that the children of today can save us from ourselves.

Garry deGrood, Pomeroy, Washington 2018.